NORMAN VINC[ENT]
PEAL[E]

Positive Power for Daily Living

NORMAN VINCENT PEALE

Positive Power for Daily Living

Copyright © 1996 Peale Foundation,
used by license agreement with Peale Center for Christian Living.

Published by Garborg's Heart 'n Home, Inc.
P. O. Box 20132, Bloomington, MN 55420

All rights reserved. No part of this book may be reproduced in any form without permission in writing from the publisher.

Unless otherwise noted, all Scripture is taken from the HOLY BIBLE, NEW INTERNATIONAL VERSION® NIV®. Copyright © 1973, 1978, 1984 by International Bible Society. All rights reserved.

Compiled by Janet L. Weaver

SPCN 5-5044-0303-0

Each day is a gift from God. This is His world we live in and He is always with us. Each day is full of great opportunities. A wonderful way to begin the day is to say this verse aloud: "This is the day the Lord has made; let us rejoice and be glad in it" (Psalm 118:24).

JANUARY 1

God established time and He didn't put a line through it. It was calendar makers who did that. Eternal life isn't off in the future somewhere. Eternal life is now. This is eternity, now, today.

God has set eternity in the hearts of men.
ECCLESIASTES 3:11

DECEMBER 31

An incredible goodness is operating on your behalf. Confidently receive God's abundant blessings. Think abundance, prosperity, and the best of everything. God wants to give you every good thing. Do not hinder His generosity.

We will shout for joy when you are victorious and will
lift up our banners in the name of our God. May
the Lord grant all your requests.

PSALM 20:5

JANUARY 2

The power of God is available to anyone and is more than equal to any problem. Time and again I've seen a single individual confront some gigantic task, take a deep breath, ask for God's help—and then go on to accomplish the seemingly impossible.

DECEMBER 30

We are all capable of greater things than we realize. How much one actually achieves depends largely on: desire, faith, persistent effort, and ability. If you are lacking in the first three factors, your ability will not count for much.

JANUARY 3

Build yourself a better future by attacking it with faith!

Fight the good fight of the faith. Take hold of the eternal life to which you were called.

1 TIMOTHY 6:12

DECEMBER 29

Success proceeds by first having a specifically sharp goal and holding it until it sinks into your unconscious. Then surround this goal with positive thought and faith, giving it positive follow-through.

Jesus replied...I tell you the truth, if you have faith and do not doubt.... If you believe, you will receive whatever you ask for in prayer.

MATTHEW 21:21,22

JANUARY 4

The big thing is your attitude toward problems... attitudes are more important than facts.... You can't ignore facts; but the attitude with which you approach the facts is all-important.

DECEMBER 28

When you get to know Jesus Christ, you will become aware of the fact that you are a child of God and that God wants you to be a creative person. He will then give you clarity so you will know exactly what you can do with this wonderful personality.

JANUARY 5

We become dull spirited when we weakly give in to various temptations.

Watch and pray so that you will not fall into temptation. The spirit is willing, but the body is weak.

MATTHEW 26:41

DECEMBER 27

The Positive thinker takes obstacles or difficulties that arise as creative opportunities...looking for ways to turn it to advantage.

And we know that in all things God works for the good of those who love him, who have been called according to his purpose.

ROMANS 8:28

JANUARY 6

True peace always comes by the surrender of self to Christ.

DECEMBER 26

When you feel inadequate and inferior in the face of dealing with other people or dealing with situations, tell yourself over and over there is power within you. Take a statement like this from the Gospel of John and embed it into your consciousness: "As many as received him, to them he gave power..." to become what? "To become sons of God."

JANUARY 7

The Christmas story was ushered in with a song: "Peace on earth, good will toward men." When we have good will in our minds, we also have peace of mind. When we have peace in our hearts, we also have love in our hearts. Who but our Lord could have thought of such a simple way to happiness?

DECEMBER 25

Change your mental habits to belief instead of disbelief.

If any of you lacks wisdom, he should ask of God, who gives generously to all.... But when he asks, he must believe and not doubt.

JAMES 1:5,6

JANUARY 8

The happy person is the person who has what it takes to fight through and not be overcome.

In this world you will have trouble. But take heart! I have overcome the world.

JOHN 16:33

DECEMBER 24

A reenergizing of the mind takes place when I remember in the problems and difficulties of daily living that I am a child of God and in Him "I live and have my being."

JANUARY 9

Events are governed by creative thoughts. Get in the habit of thinking good days and you will go a long way toward getting what you think.

DECEMBER 23

When we are wise enough to connect...with the flow of God's power, we discover that no adversity need overwhelm or defeat us.

My grace is sufficient for you, for My power is made perfect in weakness.

2 CORINTHIANS 12:9

JANUARY 10

A true friend has that fine sense of timing which enables him to say strengthening words of comfort just when they are needed.

A friend loves at all times.

PROVERBS 17:17

DECEMBER 22

The six-word affirmation: "With God all things are possible" keeps reminding us that possibilities exist, though not yet clear, and challenge us to discern and realize those possibilities with God's guidance.

JANUARY 11

Cut through your differences with people through keen intelligence and patience, emphasizing the reasons for togetherness. Find the common purpose you have with others and weld yourselves together in love.

DECEMBER 21

That which we affirm constantly has the tendency to take over in our thoughts and to produce changed attitudes.

Seven times a day I praise you...great peace have they who love your law, and nothing can make them stumble.

PSALM 119:164,165

JANUARY 12

*The power of faith is stronger
than the power of fear.*

Don't be afraid; just believe.

MARK 5:36

DECEMBER 20

You can never know what pressure motivates another person driving a car carelessly. Instead of reacting in kind, perhaps your prayer may reach his problem. One thing is sure, it will reach you.

JANUARY 13

There is a power in an individual whereby he can decide, "I will it to be. This is my decision—with the help of God." Naturally, will power is so much whistling in the dark unless you combine it with God's help.

DECEMBER 19

This country...could fade into the oblivion of history...if we get conceited and think we know more than God.

If my people, who are called by name, will humble themselves and pray and seek my face and turn from their wicked ways, then will I hear from heaven and will forgive their sin and heal their land.

2 CHRONICLES 7:14

JANUARY 14

*Always begin the day with the thought of God,
His love and care, and with the thought of
your responsibility for serving Him.*

I will sing of your strength, in the morning
I will sing of your love.

PSALM 59:16

DECEMBER 18

There is no easy religion. The benefits of religion in your life require self-discipline, the full and honest giving of self, a complete break with all wrongdoing, and a persistent and patient rehabilitation of your character. You cannot do it without the help of God.

JANUARY 15

A real and self-forgetting act of mercy that reflects the inspiration Jesus gives will create a deeper satisfaction than giving or receiving the most expensive gift.

DECEMBER 17

The American people have ever been compassionate for the less fortunate. Our traditions of freedom demand that we give succor to those who struggle for freedom.

JANUARY 16

*Know for a fact that you are never alone.
A great Someone is with you always.*

DECEMBER 16

The Biblical advice "Do not let the sun go down on your anger" is psychologically very sound. Anger can accumulate and must be emptied out every night. In prayer, drain off the anger content that may be in your mind and forgive...practice forgetting.

Forgive as the Lord forgave you.
COLOSSIANS 3:13

JANUARY 17

A child who starts out in life with a feeling of being loved and in partnership with God will know that he has undefeatable resources.

Jesus said…"Let the little children come to me, and do not hinder them, for the kingdom of God belongs to such as these."

MARK 10:14,15

DECEMBER 15

"I can do all things through Christ which strengtheneth me" (Philippians 4:13, KJV). This truth is an antidote for every defeated feeling. If you feel downed by situations and the going is hard, this statement will remind you...that Christ is with you and is now giving you all the help you need.

JANUARY 18

*Go at life with abandon; give it all you've got.
And life will give all it has to you.*

DECEMBER 14

People kill their happiness in life by their tongues.
They explode or write a sharp letter and the evil is done.
The real victim is not the other person but oneself.

Out of the same mouth come praise and cursing....
My brothers, this should not be.

JAMES 3:9,10

JANUARY 19

Worry is a destructive process of occupying the mind with thoughts contrary to God's love and care. The cure is to fill the mind with thoughts of God's power, His protection, and His goodness.

Trust in the Lord with all your heart and lean not on your own understanding; in all your ways acknowledge him, and he will make your paths straight.

PROVERBS 3:5,6

DECEMBER 13

Teach yourself to believe that through Christ's help you can do all things. As you continue this affirmation you will actually experience Christ's help. You will find yourself meeting problems with new mental force. You will carry heavy burdens with ease. Your new lifting power will amaze you.

JANUARY 20

The hope of the world is in Jesus, because He alone bridges the gap between people. He alone brings people together as brothers. A world full of Jesus is a world full of love and brotherhood.

DECEMBER 12

Faith is the antidote to worry.

O you of little faith...do not worry...
seek first his kingdom.

MATTHEW 6:30,31,33

JANUARY 21

One of the chief skills in human relations is to take every person as he is and accept him that way.

Accept one another, then, just as Christ accepted you, in order to bring praise to God.

ROMANS 15:7

DECEMBER 11

No human life, no matter what happens to it, need be defeated unless that individual accepts defeat. If you operate on the principle that "He that believeth on me, the works that I do shall he do also; and greater works than these shall he do," (John 14:12, KJV) you can work a miracle in your life.

JANUARY 22

If we accept and live by the sayings of Jesus Christ, we will become like that wise man who built his house upon the rock against which the storms beat in vain. People can feel beaten by life's difficulties, but when they listen to Christ they find inner serenity, strength, courage, and wisdom that defy all the storms of life.

DECEMBER 10

Your life is going to be no better than your attitudes are.

If anything is excellent or praiseworthy—
think about such things.

PHILIPPIANS 4:8

JANUARY 23

Wisdom is often revealed by God in the form of a sudden thought or inspiration. An entirely new idea may come as an inspiration or revelation from God.

The wisdom that comes from heaven is first of all pure; then peace-loving, considerate, submissive, full of mercy and good fruit, impartial and sincere.

JAMES 3:17

DECEMBER 9

The pressure of modern life against the inner spirit of a man is great. It is likely to have disastrous results unless we as individuals and as a nation buttress ourselves from within.... Faith can give us those inner braces.

JANUARY 24

Do your best and leave the results to God.

DECEMBER 8

A wonderful life isn't given to you by any magical means. You create it out of the way you think and the way you react.

JANUARY 25

Face your weakness, examine it, and plot a campaign to overcome it. With concentrated effort and prayer, you can become strongest in your weakest point.

The Spirit helps us in our weakness. We do not know what we ought to pray for, but the Spirit himself intercedes for us.

ROMANS 8:26

DECEMBER 7

What may seem like ingratitude in children may be a desire for self-expression crudely articulated. Young people want to think and act for themselves, even if they make mistakes in doing so. In such event parents need to pray for extra patience and understanding.

JANUARY 26

Enthusiasm is a word meaning full of God. So to have enthusiasm fill your mind full of God.

DECEMBER 6

Face the army lines of discouragement, frustration, disappointment, hostility, and weakness and visualize these enemies of your peace and happiness as retreating as you affirm, "If God is for us, who can be against us?" (Romans 8:31).

JANUARY 27

Learn to notice and appreciate the beauty of nature. There is healing for tension in getting close to nature. A few moments' contemplation of the sky can relax tension and refresh the soul.

DECEMBER 5

The future belongs always to the believers who are for something; never to those who are only against something.

Whoever hears My word and believes Him who sent me has eternal life and will not be condemned; he has crossed over from death to life.

JOHN 5:24

JANUARY 28

*Patient understanding is the secret
of all human relationships.*

Encourage the timid, help the weak, be patient with
everyone...always try to be kind to each other.

1 THESSALONIANS 5:14,15

DECEMBER 4

Difficulties are our blessings. Difficulties bring out talents. Disraeli said, "Difficulties constitute the best education in this life." Horace, the great Roman, said, "Difficulties elicit talents that in more fortunate circumstances would lie dormant."

JANUARY 29

The secret of life isn't what happens to you, but what you do with what happens to you.

DECEMBER 3

Try Prayer Power. The most important single step in facing sorrow is to ask Jesus Christ to assuage your anguish and believe that He does so.

Praise be to the God and Father of our Lord Jesus Christ, the Father of compassion and the God of all comfort, who comforts us in all our troubles.

2 CORINTHIANS 1:3

JANUARY 30

Faith teaches us how to stand up against anything... to be resilient. Realize you have within yourself what it takes to be absolutely undefeatable.

In all these things we are more than conquerors through him who loved us.

ROMANS 8:37

DECEMBER 2

To be truly educated means to have one's insights deepened—not to have one's information increased. It means to have a clear sympathetic understanding of the human race and its problems. There is nothing more sad than a person filled with "book-learning" who lacks this true awareness.

JANUARY 31

Life is but a few great experiences strung like jewels on ordinary string with routines in between. These glorious experiences can remind us of how great life is.

DECEMBER 1

The controlled person is a powerful person. He who always keeps his head will get ahead. The number of lives that have been ruined through lack of emotional control is stupendous.

FEBRUARY 1

If you take the attitude that everything is against you and it is all unfair...then you make yourself the victim of adverse circumstances. Your outlook determines your future.

NOVEMBER 30

I have discovered that the most vital, creative, and positive thoughts are those stated in the Bible. The words of the Bible are capable of revolutionizing the entire personality.

If you remain in me and my words remain in you, ask whatever you wish, and it will be given you.

JOHN 15:7

FEBRUARY 2

*Give your thoughts a good overhauling.
With God's help you can think your
way to success and real happiness.*

He who began a good work in you will carry it on
to completion until the day of Christ Jesus.

PHILIPPIANS 1:6

NOVEMBER 29

The best antidote for sorrow is affection, caring, and love. The best way to help a person in grief is to express those things in any way that you can.

FEBRUARY 3

Trust means to believe in man's finest capacities.

NOVEMBER 28

The Bible tells how to live as strong people. However, this strength is not within ourselves but in the Lord. When you are strong in the Lord, you have life's greatest strength.

> Finally, my brethren, be strong in the Lord,
> and in the power of His might.
> EPHESIANS 6:10 KJV

FEBRUARY 4

None can escape the fact that we become, to a large degree, what we think. Think little, believe little, act little, and the results will be little. Think big, believe big, act big, and the results will be big.

According to your faith will it be done to you.

MATTHEW 9:29

NOVEMBER 27

The best of all ways to get your mind off your own troubles is to try to help someone else with his.

FEBRUARY 5

To help promote tranquillity I have a technique of remembering beauty. I remember the beauty of Switzerland at evening time when the snows on the mountain change colors. I remember the nighttime mists upon the China Sea. Tranquility of mind helps us to live life calmly.

NOVEMBER 26

*Take counsel from your beliefs,
not your fears—and you
will do better in life.*

FEBRUARY 6

Fill every moment of the day with positive, joyful thoughts and your day will be full of positive, joyful living.

NOVEMBER 25

Never let yourself live with too much caution.
Throw yourself into life, even if you get hurt.

Fight the good fight of faith. Take hold of the
eternal life to which you were called.

1 TIMOTHY 6:12

FEBRUARY 7

You can change your life in any aspect by changing your thoughts about that aspect.

We have the mind of Christ.

1 CORINTHIANS 2:16

We take captive every thought to make it obedient to Christ.

2 CORINTHIANS 10:5

NOVEMBER 24

One of the problems of our day is how to counteract the effects on the next generation of a civilization dedicated to the pursuit of luxury and the avoidance of effort. We are in danger of robbing our children of their greatest heritage: the heritage of struggle.

FEBRUARY 8

On Thanksgiving Day we think especially about our country and give thanks for it. We can thank God for the greatest blessing; that is freedom under God for all men. When we give thanks for the privilege of being Americans, our collective feeling somehow enters into the national atmosphere and benefits America.

NOVEMBER 23

It takes struggle, a goal, and enthusiasm to make a champion.

I have fought the good fight, I have finished the race, I have kept the faith. Now there is in store for me the crown of righteousness.

2 TIMOTHY 4:7,8

FEBRUARY 9

Every day of your life try being thankful. There is much healing potency in the simple exercise of giving thanks.

Let them give thanks to the Lord for his unfailing love and his wonderful deeds for men, for he satisfies the thirsty and fills the hungry with good things.

PSALM 107:8,9

NOVEMBER 22

Questions and doubts mean that a child is alive; that he thinks. You cannot hand faith down in packaged form like an heirloom to your children. They must find it and develop it for themselves. He who never has to fight a doubt is not a thinker.

FEBRUARY 10

*The simple things should never be taken for granted.
They are more precious and wonderful than we think.
We should be everlastingly grateful for them.
Thankfulness to God is not a matter for Thanksgiving
Day alone, but for every day of the year.*

NOVEMBER 21

Christianity makes old creatures new. You never need to settle for what you are. You can be a new person. I've seen people change—defeated people become victorious, dull people become excited. God doesn't merely create you; He repeatedly re-creates you.

FEBRUARY 11

Make your own inventory of your everyday blessings, and then consider how terribly out of it you would be without them. You will gratefully realize how much you have to be thankful for.

NOVEMBER 20

Keep calm. Christ helps you keep calm. If you're not calm you tend to flounder, to overly press; you get off of fine balance. You are not under centralized control.

You will keep in perfect peace him whose mind
is steadfast, because he trusts in you.

ISAIAH 26:3

FEBRUARY 12

Thanksgiving is a recognition of past benefits and the activator of blessings yet to come.

You will be made rich in every way so that you can be generous on every occasion, and through us your generosity will result in thanksgiving to God.

2 CORINTHIANS 9:11

NOVEMBER 19

Often misfortune and frustration work directly to your benefit. They make you so much want a change for the better that you get busy and start trying. No one ever accomplishes anything worthwhile in life unless he has a deep desire to do so.

FEBRUARY 13

I often pray with someone over the telephone. A telephone is an instrument of communication and prayer is an act of communicating. When two or three are gathered together in His name, the Lord is in the midst of them...so together we shut our eyes and open our minds and pray for guidance.

NOVEMBER 18

When we surround children with love, faith, respect, normal attention, and cooperation, their powers flow freely and effectively.

People were bringing little children to Jesus to have him touch them...and he took the children in his arms, put his hands on them and blessed them.

MARK 10:13,16

FEBRUARY 14

The attitude of gratitude is important in achieving wholeness in life. Only by enumerating the many blessings bestowed upon us can we fully appreciate the bounty of God.

> Be joyful always; pray continually; give thanks in all circumstances, for this is God's will for you in Christ Jesus.
>
> 1 THESSALONIANS 5:16-18

NOVEMBER 17

Faith means giving thanks for the sheer wonder of the gift of life and saying to your Creator, "So long thy power hath blest me, sure it still will lead me on." It means reminding yourself that there is always light beyond the darkness even when you cannot see it.

FEBRUARY 15

A person who is free, who has found the answer to life, who is no longer a victim of his inner conflicts but is released and whole—is a success.

NOVEMBER 16

Be yourself. When we reject what makes us special, water down our God-given individuality and uniqueness, we begin to lose our freedom. The conformist is in no way a free man. He has to follow the herd.

FEBRUARY 16

Go into action! Anything you do has its risks and drawbacks. It is futile to wait for foolproof circumstances or the perfect course of action. These do not exist.

Prepare your minds for action; be self-controlled; set your hope fully on the grace to be given you when Jesus Christ is revealed.

1 PETER 1:13

NOVEMBER 15

By the power of choice you can make your life creative or you can destroy it...no choice is altogether small, for upon the most seemingly unimportant choice may ultimately depend the outcome of your life.

Now choose life, so that you and your children may live...for the Lord is your life.

DEUTERONOMY 30:19,20

FEBRUARY 17

The more we put mental powers against seemingly hopeless difficulties and follow the flashes of insight which come from real thinking, the more we develop the secret of success. Such thinking gives one the daring to do the unusual when a situation calls for it.

NOVEMBER 14

Before this day is out, do something specific and concrete that will demonstrate your determination to change yourself and your life for the better. Pay a debt. Heal a broken relationship. End a quarrel. Offer an apology. Pray for someone...do whatever you do quietly, without ostentation...do it simply because you prefer to be an inner-directed person.

FEBRUARY 18

*Know that you are yourself a miracle.
And believe you can make miracles happen
by thinking, praying, believing, working,
and by helping people.*

NOVEMBER 13

Genuine Christian experience so acts upon man's mind...so that even in trouble, adversity, and pain his inner song sings on.

You are my hiding place; you will protect me from trouble and surround me with songs of deliverance.

PSALM 32:7

FEBRUARY 19

If you are weak, tired, sick, defeated, unhappy...you can be resurrected. Jesus is still healing and changing people all over the world. He can change you now. Once the resurrection power of Jesus Christ takes ahold of you; you become strong.

Jesus said to her, "I am the resurrection and the life, he who believes in me will live, even though he dies."

JOHN 11:25

NOVEMBER 12

The individual who is truly alive practices innovation—that is he substitutes the new for the old. As a person becomes older the tendency is to believe that the values, customs, and procedures of the past are inherently sacred. But they aren't necessarily so. They should be questioned and requestioned.

FEBRUARY 20

Spiritual rebirth is vital to joy and peace. Christianity is not a doctrine of escape from the harsh aspects of life, but victory over them. Sacrifice, itself, is the deepest joy.

NOVEMBER 11

Jesus...came as the greatest revolutionary who ever lived. He brought the revolutionary doctrine of love, character, and manhood.

Love the Lord your God with all your heart and with all your soul and with all your mind and with all your strength.... Love your neighbor as yourself.

MARK 12:30,31

FEBRUARY 21

Simply being with a person who is bereaved will give him more solace and comfort than you know. It shows him that you care.

Blessed are those who mourn, for they will be comforted.

MATTHEW 5:4

NOVEMBER 10

If we are to survive as a nation and discharge our leadership in the complex world, we and our leaders need to depend upon the guidance of God as did our forefathers in their time.

FEBRUARY 22

Contact with God establishes within us a flow of the same type of energy that re-creates the world and renews springtime every year.

NOVEMBER 9

The genius of Christianity is that it teaches us to laugh through tears; it teaches us to have sunlight in darkness.... It is hope as contrasted with despair; it is victory as contrasted with defeat. It is the most... dynamic force ever to come into human history.

FEBRUARY 23

Develop a thankful disposition and you become a happier person.

He who sacrifices thank offerings honors me, and he prepares the way so that I may show him the salvation of God.

PSALM 50:23

NOVEMBER 8

Christianity is more than a creed.... It is a pulsating, vibrant, creative energy...a deep therapy which can drive to the heart of a personality, endowing it with new energy—in a word, re-creating.

Create in me a pure heart, O God, and renew
a steadfast spirit within me.

PSALM 51:10

FEBRUARY 24

If we put ourselves in God's hands and are spiritually changed, "times of refreshing shall come from the presence of the Lord." How clean, fresh, and delightful life then becomes! It is the same kind of experience as falling in love, only deeper and more profound... it is called "spiritual awakening."

NOVEMBER 7

There is no situation so completely hopeless
that something constructive cannot be done about it.
When life hands you a lemon, make lemonade.

FEBRUARY 25

Pain is a part of life in this world. God is your Father and comforts you when you are hurt and helps you to be happy again.

The Father of compassion and the God of all comfort, who comforts us in all our troubles.

2 CORINTHIANS 1:3,4

NOVEMBER 6

One of the principal ways children learn is by making mistakes. Depriving a child of the chance to make his own mistakes robs him of the chance to grow.

FEBRUARY 26

Very often, after some great emotional experience, there is a need to be alone. To relive and rethink the experience. To determine how it has changed things, and ponder what those changes mean. To allow the drained mind and the exhausted spirit to regain poise and strength.

NOVEMBER 5

We most truly honor Christ when we live the example He set.

Whoever has my commands and obeys them, he is the one who loves me. He who loves me will be loved by my Father, and I too will love him and show myself to him.

JOHN 14:21

FEBRUARY 27

With so much tension in modern life, one must occasionally retreat from the world in order to live in the world.

Because so many people were coming and going...they did not even have a chance to eat...so they went away by themselves in a boat to a solitary place.

MARK 6:31,32

NOVEMBER 4

It is my belief that money used with little or no concern for God or humanity is sour money and will go bad. But money used with spiritual responsibility is good money and will continue to flow abundantly in the prosperity-supply pattern.

FEBRUARY 28

During the last hour before retiring, deliberately prevent the mind from being agitated by problems. The cares, responsibilities, and decisions of life should be put aside for the night so that mind, soul, and body may be refreshed and renewed by sound, healthful sleep.

NOVEMBER 3

I am impressed by people and their astounding ability to meet tough situations. One man who had experienced one defeat after another declared, "I find that God has built a come-back capacity into me." How right he is.

With your help I can advance against a troop; with my God I can scale a wall. It is God who arms me with strength and makes my way perfect.

PSALM 18:29,32

FEBRUARY 29

Continual sinning "hardens the heart" and eventually closes off forgiveness—not because God withdraws it, but because we become incapable of receiving it.

NOVEMBER 2

Many barriers between people are due to non-listening. The sun rises and sets daily on numberless conversations leading exactly nowhere, because people are so taken with their own preconceived ideas that the other fellow's views never register.

MARCH 1

Sin requires only a moment to happen and what happens can make you miserable for years.

I have hidden your word in my heart that
I might not sin against you.

PSALM 119:11

NOVEMBER 1

When the mind is agitated by the noise, hurry, and confusion of modern life, you cannot consult the creative depths within yourself for answers to your perplexing problems.

Be still and know that I am God.

PSALM 46:10

MARCH 2

The problem of helping people to like you may be as simple as helping them to learn to like themselves and recover their faith.

OCTOBER 31

The spiritual experience of surrendering one's self to God by an act of faith and a wholehearted readiness to follow God's will drives deeply into the personality, releasing the hidden energies to produce a person of wisdom and power.

MARCH 3

Creative silence is an element in which fresh inspiration comes. Spiritual quietness is a source of right solutions and new starts. How can you consult the creative depths within yourself for valid answers when your mind is agitated by noise, hurry, and confusion of modern life?

He leads me beside quiet waters, he restores my soul.

PSALM 23:1,2

OCTOBER 30

The color of a man's skin has no bearing upon his desirability as a neighbor. The only proper standard of judgment is how he conducts himself.

MARCH 4

If you have had some contact with God, share it with someone else. If you do so, you will feel your heart warmed and filled with His presence. It should be natural to share your richest experiences of God with others. He walks and talks with all who live naturally with Him.

OCTOBER 29

When the hidden energies of the subconscious are brought under the influence of Christ as Master of life, the most amazing results appear in lives hitherto commonplace or defeated.

We demolish arguments and every pretension that sets itself up against the knowledge of God, and we take captive every thought and make it obedient to Christ.

2 CORINTHIANS 10:5

MARCH 5

Self-control is healthy spiritually, physically, and mentally. When you firmly decide to maintain your ideals, strength to do so will come to you through prayer.

OCTOBER 28

There is one way to avoid criticism: Never do anything, never amount to anything. Never get your head above the crowd so the jealous will notice and attack you. Criticism is a sign that your personality has some force.

MARCH 6

Unselfish love does not come naturally to anybody—it is something a person has to learn, practice, and cultivate—but it is the only way we find abiding happiness.

May the Lord direct your hearts into
God's love and Christ's perseverance.

2 THESSALONIANS 3:5

OCTOBER 27

The chief emblem of Christianity is the Cross, a symbol of suffering. But in a higher sense the Cross is the symbol of glorious victory. Faith in the Cross of Christ gives victory, cleanness, and a release from sin that is joy indescribable.

MARCH 7

Faith is the most powerful of all forces in humanity, and when you have it in depth, nothing can get you down. Nothing.

OCTOBER 26

When you attack boldly in support of the right as you see it, creative and spiritual forces will indeed come to your aid. You will have support and strength you would not have believed possible.

Judgment will again be founded on righteousness, and all the upright in heart will follow it.

PSALM 94:15

MARCH 8

Do not be awestruck by other people and do not try to copy them. Nobody can be you as well as YOU can.

I praise you because I am fearfully and wonderfully made; your works are wonderful, I know that full well.

PSALM 139:14

OCTOBER 25

Moments may come when courage alone shall stand between us and disaster. What is the source of such rugged courage? That sense of God's presence when we hear Him say, "I am with you always."

MARCH 9

The best sermon is just being a good example, because it is wordless and therefore doesn't arouse the antagonism that the voice of authority often does.

OCTOBER 24

The mental climate a person creates determines whether they will have confidence even when things seem hopeless, have courage even when apprehensive factors appear, or live in fear because of an attitude of hopelessness and apprehension.

The Lord is the stronghold of my life—
of whom shall I be afraid?

PSALM 27:1

MARCH 10

If you run in fear, you literally run yourself down.

Stand firm and see the deliverance the Lord will give you...do not be afraid; do not be discouraged. Go out to face them tomorrow, and the Lord will be with you.

2 CHRONICLES 20:17

OCTOBER 23

Courtesy has an amazing power to dissipate ill will. By practicing a generous and forbearing attitude, you can finally lift kindliness into affection—and from that to the ultimate in personal relationships: Where you put the other person ahead of yourself.

MARCH 11

The secret of self-confidence and courage hinges on the kind of thoughts you think. In the long run, your subconscious will send up to you exactly what you send down to it. Take charge of your mind and begin to fill it with healthy thoughts. The Bible is full of healing thoughts which will fill you with courage and self-confidence.

OCTOBER 22

Ask yourself honestly what there is in you that is sore to the touch of life. Ask God to put some healing balm on that sore spot until it heals. Open your mind and let the grievance flow out. Go to someone you trust and pour it our until not a vestige of it remains within you.

MARCH 12

Difficulties must be studied and efficiently dealt with to be eliminated, but they must be seen only for what they are. They must not be inflated by fear.

The Lord is the stronghold of my life—of whom shall I be afraid? Though an army besiege me, my heart will not fear; though war break out against me, even then will I be confident.

PSALM 27:1,3

OCTOBER 21

Pray for courage. I believe a person should pray for courage as he prays for his daily bread. God will give it to you, because He will give you himself.

Then Jesus declared, "I am the bread of life. He who comes to me will never go hungry, and he who believes in me will never be thirsty."

JOHN 6:35

MARCH 13

The basis for confidence in yourself is simply to realize that you are a child of God and that "the kingdom of God is within you." This means that within you is a rich vein of understanding, insight, and strength for surmounting difficulties and attaining goals.

OCTOBER 20

When we repent of our sins and ask God's forgiveness, He grants it. Then we must believe we are forgiven and practice self-forgiveness. Simply say, "I forgive myself; my sin is ended." In time your feeling of guilt about past sins will leave you, provided you continue to live right.

MARCH 14

Christianity still maintains its ancient power in the world because there are always people who find out that these things are true.

Heaven and earth will pass away, but my words will never pass away.

LUKE 21:33

OCTOBER 19

When the going is hard, when difficulties mount up, when the stresses are great, when the resistance is overwhelming, Christianity tells us that through faith in God and through commitment to Jesus Christ we have within us all that is needed to handle anything that is outside us.

The one who is in you is greater than
the one who is in the world.

1 JOHN 4:4

MARCH 15

Enthusiasm is not a sweet, pollyannish concept. It is a strong, rugged mental attitude that is hard to achieve, difficult to maintain, but powerful—so powerful.

OCTOBER 18

The way to stop doing something that you know to be bad is to really want to. When you develop a desire for right action that is stronger than your weakness, you will then have sufficient moral force to change.

MARCH 16

In all life there exists the mountain peaks as well as the valleys; periods of ups and downs are always present. All life has its rhythm. The fullness of life is achieved when life's rhythm is attuned to the rhythm of God.

OCTOBER 17

Acknowledge honestly what present difficulties are too much and ask for the power you need. "Cast thy burden upon the Lord," says Psalm 55 (KJV), "and He shall sustain thee." This really works! It is in no sense theoretical.

MARCH 17

*Real riches are not external or material riches.
Real riches are spiritual and internal in nature.
They are riches that no man can take away.*

Do not store up for yourselves treasures on
earth...but store up for yourselves treasures
in heaven...for where your treasure is,
there your heart will be also.

MATTHEW 6:19,20,21

OCTOBER 16

Many people repeatedly defeat themselves by insisting on handling all problems on their own. All of us do have a measure of personal power, but situations will come which we cannot handle without power from a higher source.

If any of you lacks wisdom, he should ask God, who
gives generously to all without finding fault,
and it will be given to him.

JAMES 1:5

MARCH 18

A salesman who began to see customers as people, as human beings in need of his help, actually got to loving them. People always respond to somebody who loves and tries to help them.

OCTOBER 15

Our crisis times call for people who will respond positively to challenges with a "Here-am-I-send-me" and then wade in. Such people can bring about important changes in situations and thereby set in motion forces that make for corresponding changes in the world at large.

MARCH 19

*Train yourself to look for the best in people.
People are wonderful, if you think they are.*

In humility consider others better than yourselves.

PHILIPPIANS 2:3

OCTOBER 14

*Always start the day with prayer.
It is the greatest of all mind conditioners.
Even if you do not have the time, pray
anyway. It is that important.*

Pray in the Spirit on all occasions with all kinds
of prayers and requests. With this in mind, be
alert and always keep on praying.

EPHESIANS 6:18

MARCH 20

Christianity teaches that the human soul that is identified with God lives forever. The preaching of the resurrection of Jesus Christ from the dead is the thing that gives Christianity the power to change the world.

OCTOBER 13

An experience in which you don't make out too well can shake your confidence in yourself; and if you do not promptly make another try, a defeat psychologically can take hold and freeze you. So when you fall flat—pick yourself up fast and go right on to the next challenge.

MARCH 21

You do not need to feel that you, with your own inadequate strength, must deal with everything that gangs up on you. Yield it to God. Surrender it to Him and put it in His hands. He will overcome for you that mass of difficulties that seem to have you defeated.

Show the wonder of your great love, you who save
by your right hand those who take refuge in you.

PSALM 17:7

OCTOBER 12

Depression often comes from the resentments, failures, and fears which rise out of the deep unconscious, a repository of attitudes that plague us. But God also presides in the unconscious and nothing can stand before the power of God. Faith is more powerful than fear.

MARCH 22

It is always beneficial to pull up to a higher standard and hold yourself there. Keep a resolution and carry it out one day at a time. Ask God for help every morning and thank Him every night.

OCTOBER 11

Before you go to sleep run over your personal world in your mind, thanking God for everyone and everything. Count your blessings and name them. This will nullify your complaints and cancel out discouragement.

On my bed I remember you; I think of you
through the watches of the night.

PSALM 63:6

MARCH 23

I am confident that there must be more to salvation than the exclusive doctrines of any one religious body. God's overall plan of salvation is much broader and more vast and merciful than many pious, well-intentioned people have imagined it to be.

OCTOBER 10

In marriage relationships, the mystic process of love attracts people to each other. The processes of reason, common sense, and wisdom gained from knowledge are essential to make the union a continuing success.

MARCH 24

The power of a life that is in God and the strength of a life dedicated to Jesus Christ produces a spiritual momentum to overcome big obstacles or any "giants" you may be up against. Make use of your momentum.

You armed me with strength for battle; you
made my adversaries bow at my feet.

PSALM 18:39

OCTOBER 9

If you live closely with God until you actually know Him and feel His presence, all fear passes away and a calm, quiet confidence comes.

Blessed are those who have learned to acclaim you, who walk in the light of your presence, O Lord.

PSALM 89:15

MARCH 25

The relaxed man is the powerful man. The rigid, tied-up personality is a defeated man. He does not have capacity for the give-and-take of circumstance, nor the element that gives buoyancy and flexibility with which to ride out the storms of life.

OCTOBER 8

In this world of mortality Easter comes with its glorious message that when mortal life is finished here in Christ, greater glories open up than we ever dreamed of; where there is no emphasis on decay and death, but only life and hope, of which Easter is the symbol.

MARCH 26

The dreariness of life will depart if you learn the secret of finding your happiness in human service.

Do not forget to do good and to share with others, for with such sacrifices God is pleased.

HEBREWS 13:16

OCTOBER 7

Christ recognized the difficulty we have in learning to forgive when He said to forgive seventy times seven if necessary. Literally that means 490 times. I predict that long before you forgive another person 490 times, you will be free of all resentment.

MARCH 27

Toughness of spirit in a person can overcome anything. You can get anything you want from life, but you may have to struggle for it, you may have to overcome all kinds of adversity.

OCTOBER 6

Easter turns all our sunsets into sunrise.

But God raised [Jesus] from the dead, freeing him from the agony of death, because it was impossible for death to keep its hold on him...therefore my heart is glad and my tongue rejoices; my body also will live in hope.

ACTS 2:24,26

MARCH 28

The optimist tends to throw his all into a proposition. The pessimist holds something of himself back and gets less in return than the man who gives more of himself. This explains why relaxed optimistic people achieve more than tense pessimistic people.

OCTOBER 5

The world needs millions of acts of forgiveness and repentance to flush out hate, resentment, and bitterness.

MARCH 29

In time of discouragement it helps to remember the beautiful things in your own life and in the world around you.

That I may...gaze upon the beauty of the Lord and seek him in his temple. For in the day of trouble he will keep me safe in his dwelling.

PSALM 27:4,5

OCTOBER 4

We come from God; He is our home.
Every human life feels the tug of God.

In him we live and move and have our
being...we are his offspring.

ACTS 17:28

JUNE 29

Our country came together like none other. It was born of two streams of thought: the Greek philosophers' belief in the sacredness and viability of the human mind and of the Judeo-Christian ethic dedicated to the principle that all men are the immortal children of God.

JULY 4

The opposite of error is truth. Jesus said, "I am the way, the truth and the life." When you follow Him you get yourself filled with truth. The more truth you have, the fewer bad days you will have.

JUNE 30

The Christian religion is adherence to Jesus Christ, and Him crucified. It is your relationship to a person, not to an idea, formula, creed, or tradition but to a person. When you get this person in your life, then life glows.

Jesus answered, "I am the way, the truth and the life."

JOHN 14:6

JULY 3

A lost battle doesn't mean the whole war is lost. With God's help you can take any setback or defeat and in time see it averaged out in the total pattern of your life.

He ransoms me unharmed from the battle waged
against me, even though many oppose me.

PSALM 55:18

MARCH 30

The Scriptures are full of comfort, strength and understanding. Saturate yourself in them. They are spiritual medicine, healing wounded minds and hearts.

OCTOBER 3

Robert Frost once wrote, "I'd like to get away from earth awhile. And then come back to it and begin over." That is what effectual fervent prayer does for us. It lifts us up way from our weaknesses, changes our inner state, and we emerge from it in condition for a new beginning.

MARCH 31

It is possible for every person to be alone for at least ten minutes every day to open himself to God, turn his mind to Christ, and withdraw from the busy world into a few minutes of communion that will give calm strength for the day.

Come with me by yourselves to a
quiet place and get some rest.

MARK 6:31

OCTOBER 2

Easter says to all of us, "Do not be afraid, because you have life that is forever new." People who were dead in their thoughts, dead in their hates, dead in their sins or defeats have come alive when they found Christ.

APRIL 1

Every individual must be permitted to develop his mind and soul and spirit. This is the inalienable right of the human soul. Relationships, especially those in marriage, should never seek to dominate the other as a personal possession.

OCTOBER 1

Jesus was resurrected from the dead and He said that we, too, can be. Resurrection does not only mean life after physical death, resurrection means now!

Jesus said...I am the resurrection and the life, he who believes in me will live, even though he dies; and whoever lives and believes in me will never die.

JOHN 11:25,26

APRIL 2

Marriage is an adjustment, an acquired skill in human relationships, and it requires strategy, study, and prayer.

SEPTEMBER 30

Jesus told His disciples to take the bread and wine in remembrance of His promise that He would always be with them in fellowship. Thus a comradeship was established that has endured through all centuries and is still symbolized at the holy table.

APRIL 3

No matter what life has done, no matter what you have done; there is renewal power within you. There are still vast, undamaged areas within yourself upon which you can rebuild life through God's spiritual power.

You have made known to me the path of life; you will fill me with joy in your presence, with eternal pleasures at your right hand.

PSALM 16:11

SEPTEMBER 29

Real forgiveness involves no holding back at all. One must go the whole distance in restoring relationships; and if one says, "I will forgive you the wrong you have done me but never can I forget it," that is only qualified forgiveness. To make it real forgiveness, forgetting must be added.

APRIL 4

"Forgetting those things which are behind." This is one of the greatest arts known to man. Make this day a turning point toward a new and better life for you by putting frustrations, disappointments, and painful memories out of mind. Walk away from them and forget them by giving them to God and trusting in His love, His providence, His guidance.

SEPTEMBER 28

The wide open tomb...where the stone was "rolled away" reminds us that crucifixion and death have not triumphed, but resurrection and life have won the victory. Christ, who emerged from that tomb, promised that we might share with Him the blessings of immortality. "Because I live," He said, "you will live also."

APRIL 5

Fears accompany excessive thinking about oneself. When a man gets his mind on God, he gets it off himself. Engage in less introspection if you wish to eliminate fear from your life.

When I am afraid, I will trust in you. In God, whose word I praise, in God I trust; I will not be afraid.

Psalm 56:3,4

SEPTEMBER 27

It is never necessary to compromise one's beliefs in order to get ahead. A person should be himself at all times. He should be directed by his inner convictions, not by external pressures.

Therefore, my dear brothers, stand firm. Let nothing move you. Always give yourselves fully to the work of the Lord, because you know that your labor in the Lord is not in vain.

1 CORINTHIANS 15:58

APRIL 6

Every man is the unique creation of God, created to live a life characterized by joy, energy, and vitality— to succeed in all areas of life.

So God created man in his own image, in the image of God he created him; male and female he created them.

GENESIS 1:27

SEPTEMBER 26

To all Christians, Easter brings a two-fold promise. It gives the promise of God's presence here and now to help us meet life and grow in understanding—and it gives the joyous prospect that the Lord will be with us, and we with Him, in the life hereafter.

APRIL 7

Enthusiasm smashes barriers and turns life's storms into strong tail winds that put go-ahead force behind lives. Choose enthusiasm daily and you are likely to have it permanently.

SEPTEMBER 25

Through His grace God changes men's lives: from fear to faith, from hate to love, from defeat to victory. Man must completely surrender every area of his life to God for such great changes to take place.

APRIL 8

Other things pass away, but love contains the element of eternity. It is the one sure way in which we may clearly comprehend life and its deeper mysteries.

You, being rooted and established in love, may have power...to grasp how wide and long and high and deep is the love of Christ.

EPHESIANS 3:17,18

SEPTEMBER 24

Within you is a sleeping giant—the great person you have in you to become. Keep on believing that with God's help you do have the power to beat back circumstance.

With God we will gain the victory, and he will trample down our enemies.

PSALM 60:12

APRIL 9

We have much to be thankful for, but gratitude, like affection, is not much good unless expressed. When we go to church, when we sing hymns of praise, when we kneel and thank God for His amazing gift of life, we give our spirits room to grow and expand.

SEPTEMBER 23

God's existence becomes real through personal spiritual experience. The order of our universe is powerful indication of a Supreme being. Order always indicates intelligence, and it is impossible to conceive of intelligence apart from personality.

APRIL 10

No matter what other abilities and qualities we may possess, how profound our knowledge, how great our achievements, if we do not have love none of these are of value. If we have love it adds the quality of greatness to our lives.

SEPTEMBER 22

Never has the power Jesus gave His first disciples been withdrawn from us who are His disciples today. We, too, possess His power when we have faith and humility.

But you will receive power when the Holy Spirit
comes on you; and you will be my witnesses...
to the ends of the earth.

ACTS 1:8

APRIL 11

No one can live successfully in this world who doesn't have a place of quietness within.

I do not concern myself with great matters or things too wonderful for me. But I have stilled and quieted my soul...

PSALM 131:1,2

SEPTEMBER 21

There is an ebb and flow in the tide of human life. When everything goes against you, and it seems you cannot hold on a minute longer, never give up. The tide will turn.

APRIL 12

You are a child of God and spiritual power is available for you. To have it, love God. To have it, love Jesus. To have it, love people. I doubt if any man or woman can ever get spiritual power and happiness without loving people.

SEPTEMBER 20

Remember Edison's remark: "If we did all the things we are capable of doing we would literally astonish ourselves." Astonish yourself.

APRIL 13

The whole secret of Christianity is to give. Give yourself, give your money, your time, your thought, and do it with abandon. If you give you will receive—and the more you give, the more you will receive.

Give, and it will be given to you. A good measure, pressed down, shaken together and running over, will be poured into your lap.

LUKE 6:38

SEPTEMBER 19

I have discovered among my fellow men that they have poise, peace, and happiness when they gave love rather than ill will, no matter what indignities they've been subjected to.

When they hurled their insults at him, he did not retaliate, when he suffered, he made no threats. Instead, he entrusted himself to him who judges justly.

1 PETER 2:23

APRIL 14

Jesus is the most exciting person who ever lived. He is full of vitality. He is full of romance and delight. He has never grown old. People who accept Him and build their lives around Him likewise never grow old. They remain alive to their fingertips all the days of their lives.

SEPTEMBER 18

All accomplishments, actions, and fears are stimulated first by dreams. Dreams, hopes, and desires are the roots of creativity. They keep people...alive.

APRIL 15

I am still absolutely convinced that if a person would surrender to Jesus Christ and adopt strong, affirmative attitudes toward life, he would be able to live abundantly and triumphantly.

I am come that they might have life, and that they might have it more abundantly.

JOHN 10:10 KJV

SEPTEMBER 17

*A vital part of the happiness formula is self-discipline.
Whoever conquers himself knows a deep happiness
that fills the heart with joy.*

He who ignores discipline comes to poverty and shame,
but whoever heeds correction is honored.

PROVERBS 13:18

APRIL 16

The truly spiritual person is a realist. He does not wink at facts. He looks them in the face, however dismal. This he can do serenely, for he knows that each dark situation has its bright side, and God's providence is always inherent in difficulty.

SEPTEMBER 16

The word "enthusiasm," from the Greek "entheos" means God in you, or full of God. When we claim the power of enthusiasm to work miracles in solving problems, we are actually saying that God himself in you supplies the wisdom, courage, strategy, and faith necessary to deal with all difficulties.

APRIL 17

Condition yourself to quietness. Drop your problems into a deep pool of than mental and spiritual silence and meditate upon God's peace rather than upon the specific details of the problem. This will help clarify your thinking, and before leaving that quiet place an answer may begin to emerge that proves to be the right one.

SEPTEMBER 15

We are not to fight back but love our enemies and treat kindly those who mistreat us. This is probably one of life's greatest inner struggles. But the happiness to be found in overcoming far outbalances the sadistic pleasure of hostility.

Love your enemies and pray for those
who persecute you.
MATTHEW 5:44

APRIL 18

*We are so accustomed to being alive we take it for granted.
But life is such a tremendous thing, such a privilege,
that it is cause for deep thanksgiving.*

Know that the Lord is God. It is he who made us,
and we are his; we are his people, the sheep of his pasture.
Enter his gates with thanksgiving and his courts with praise;
give thanks to him and praise his name.

PSALM 100:3,4

SEPTEMBER 14

Having enthusiasm in life is as simple as this: Cultivate the ability to love living. Love people, love the sky under which you live, love beauty, love God. The person who loves becomes enthusiastic.

APRIL 19

To win in this life you have to give every bit of yourself. Get release from self-doubt and then throw you entire self in the struggle to reach your goal. Life cannot deny itself to the person who gives life everything.

SEPTEMBER 13

You can build up your moral resistance with spiritual exercise. Then when the moral pressures of life come, gradually or suddenly, you'll not only be able to endure them, but actually be stronger by enduring them.

APRIL 20

*You will never be spiritually blessed until you forgive.
This is a basic spiritual law. Good will cannot
flow toward you unless it flows from you.*

For if you forgive men when they sin against you, your heavenly
Father will also forgive you. But if you do not forgive men
their sins, your Father will not forgive your sins.

MATTHEW 6:14,15

SEPTEMBER 12

Just as deliberate wrongdoing loads a person with invisible chains of guilt, so conscious right doing liberates creative energy.

Create in me a pure heart, O God, and renew a steadfast spirit within me.

PSALM 51:10

APRIL 21

Limitation is not put on us by God. It is self-imposed. There is a spiritual giant within each of us telling us we need not remain enslaved by weakness or victimized by frustrating limitations. The giant within you is always struggling to burst his way out of the prison you have made for him.

SEPTEMBER 11

The great moral yardsticks that God offers are the Ten Commandments and the Golden Rule. Philosophers of all ages have tried to improve on them without much success.

APRIL 22

There is no better way of living every day
to its fullest than by leaving both yesterday
and tomorrow in God's hands.

SEPTEMBER 10

Wait upon the Lord until He gives you the strength to eliminate fear, guilt, and self-pity…then your power will be replenished. Let Christ do a revitalizing job on you. Wait upon the Lord until you get the determination to do things.

Those who hope in the Lord will renew their strength.
ISAIAH 40:31

APRIL 23

The main avenue into the kingdom of God is for a person to absorb and live the Spirit of Jesus Christ.

When the Counselor comes, whom I will send to you from the Father, the Spirit of truth who goes out from the Father, he will testify about me.

JOHN 14:26

SEPTEMBER 9

Human society is not destroyed by bombs falling from the sky...it is destroyed by the decay of ideals. It is the slow, steady deterioration of our faith, the breaking and crumbling of our morals, that can destroy us as a people.

APRIL 24

Try to consider criticism objectively. Try to profit by it, even when it is unfriendly. A critic is an asset, even though an unpleasant one.

SEPTEMBER 8

An adult cannot be rocked to sleep in a mother's arms—so one of the subtlest transferences is from mother's arms to God's arms. The sense of divine support and comfort so received is essential to relaxation in its deepest meaning.

APRIL 25

The kingdom of God is within you—within every man. It is God's gift to all humanity—available for the asking.

Seek first his kingdom and his righteousness.

MATTHEW 6:33

SEPTEMBER 7

You get enthusiasm by developing a sensitive responsiveness to the world and to life—an inner awareness and excitement about the glory of life.

I have come that they may have life,
and have it to the full.

JOHN 10:10

APRIL 26

It is wonderful to be needed and to serve others. Unfortunately in this day and age some people are too busy building walls around themselves. But when the chips are down, people still need people. Don't shut yourself out from a rare and beautiful thing... take time to be a friend.

SEPTEMBER 6

Life will never lose its romance for the person who, unselfishly, does good for people.

Therefore, as we have opportunity, let us do good to all people, especially to those who belong to the family of believers.

GALATIANS 6:10

APRIL 27

Take good care of your family—they, too, are your fellow men. Only those who do the thing at hand effectively can expect to serve well in broader fields.

SEPTEMBER 5

When you "incline your ear," that is, lean earnestly toward God and really listen, God's truth will penetrate the control center of your life. Indeed, you will experience such quality and intensity of life that your soul will live in depth.

APRIL 28

Kindness is an old basic law of life that always gains good results. Be kind to one another, for kindness works wonders, makes one happy inside, and gives power and delight on the outside.

The fruit of the Spirit is love, joy, peace, patience, kindness, goodness, faithfulness, gentleness and self-control. Against such things there is no law.

GALATIANS 5:22

SEPTEMBER 4

A mind full of gloomy foreboding thoughts makes difficult the cheerful and spirited quality of thinking that stimulates enthusiasm. Mental ventilation reconditions the mind to accept the creative thought climate in which enthusiasm may develop and finally become the dominant factor.

Be transformed by the renewing of your mind.

ROMANS 12:2

APRIL 29

Standing solitary and alone, like some impregnable Mount Everest, Jesus Christ towers over the landscape of human life and history. In every time, in every era, men have gazed in admiration and awe at the colossal figure of the Nazarene.
He is the sensation of the ages.

SEPTEMBER 3

When error is in the saddle and rides us, we do things that we spend much time regretting. When truth is in control, we stay on the beam and handle life's problems masterfully.

APRIL 30

God says to us that no matter how deficient, how defective, how hateful, how sin-filled our lives may have become, they can be raised up into newness of life by the risen Christ.

I will give you a new heart and put a new spirit in you;
I will remove from you your heart of stone and
give you a heart of flesh.

EZEKIEL 36:26

SEPTEMBER 2

The beauty and inspiration of nature are part of God's healing process. The endless galaxies of innumerable stars; the tempestuous oceans; great sighing, surging winds; dashing rain; the drama of the recurring seasons: what a stupendous framework God provides as a setting for a person's life.

MAY 1

The great secret of more joy in living is through spiritual inspiration and development of vital faith. A lot more joy in living can be yours if you fully open yourself to it.

SEPTEMBER 1

Escapism can destroy you. It may not kill you physically, but it will cost you your finest possibilities in life and, eventually, your peace of mind.

Therefore, put on the full armor of God, so that when the day of evil comes, you may be able to stand your ground, and after you have done everything, to stand.

EPHESIANS 6:13

MAY 2

A lifetime on this wonderful earth doesn't last very long. It is here today and gone tomorrow, so love while you can.

AUGUST 31

Negative feelings such as fear, hate, and guilt give rise to tensions that become continuous, preventing adequate relaxation between peaks of activity. Eventually they can so impair resiliency that daily pressures are unbearable. Determine to go to work on these "negatives" and root them out.

MAY 3

Jesus sees every person as a human being whom He loves. He preserves the human essence. He emphasizes the individual worth. He tells us we all have talents. And that is why we love Him.

Having loved his own...he now showed
them the full extent of his love.

JOHN 13:1

AUGUST 30

It is not God's plan to keep sorrow from us, but He does help us meet and overcome it.

As servants of God we commend ourselves in every way... known, yet regarded as unknown; dying, and yet we live on; beaten, and yet not killed; sorrowful, yet always rejoicing.

2 CORINTHIANS 6:4,9,10

MAY 4

I have never departed from the conviction that if I live the committed life and try to serve other people I will be effective. If, in this way, a preacher can be effective; a layman can be doubly effective because a preacher is expected to live this way, while everyone is pleasantly surprised when a layman does.

AUGUST 29

Take a creative attitude toward misguided persons involved in sin and evil. Always send out a prayer for their redemption. See people in terms not of what they are but what, by God's grace, they can become. This form of spiritual concern can set in motion vital spiritual forces to combat the forces of evil now running amuck in people's lives.

MAY 5

To the extent that you deeply believe in God will you develop inner quietness and be established by assurance.

Have faith in the Lord your God
and you will be upheld.

2 CHRONICLES 20:20

AUGUST 28

Set aside a few minutes to think about Jesus, to confess sins, to pray for those who have done wrong against you, and to ask for strength. If you do this consistently day after day, a true faith will begin to send spiritual health and power through your personality.

MAY 6

When you face a mess of difficulties, it can be plenty tough. But if you adopt the outlook that something great can be done with your trouble, you can do something great.

AUGUST 27

Faith in God gives a person faith in himself, faith in his fellow men, faith in the future. When you put on faith, you put on bright glasses which enable you to see new possibilities; and you look at difficulties with new eyes.

Now faith is being sure of what we hope for and certain of what we do not see.

HEBREWS 11:1

MAY 7

Jesus is the most scintillating, dynamic, and powerful personality that history ever produced. Never in all of the history of mankind was there such a brain, such penetration, such clarity of thought, such rare gifts of insight. He has love for people and a strange, mysterious power to change them. One day we accept Him and we are changed.

AUGUST 26

The prophet Ezekiel was taken out by the Lord and shown a wide valley full of dry bones. Dramatically they came together as life was renewed in them and a great host of living men marched out of the valley of death. This Biblical incident reminds us that the dead bones of our lives shall live again—that when God's Spirit comes upon us, that which is harmonious with His Spirit shall live in us.

MAY 8

Make a mental list of the numerous times God has been good to you. Then affirm, "Since God has helped me so many times, I will continue to count upon His amazing kindness." Repeat this practice daily and you will be amazed by the new tranquillity of your mind.

Taste and see that the Lord is good.

PSALM 34:8

AUGUST 25

There is a force more powerful than fear, and that is faith. When fear comes to your mind counter it with an affirmation of faith.

Continue in your faith, established and firm, not moved from the hope held out in the gospel.

COLOSSIANS 1:23

MAY 9

Jealousy has two roots: abnormal self-centeredness and insecurity. Fear of being forsaken and left alone lies at the root of this. The antidote for this is faith. Faith will enhance your own attractive and unique personality and keep you inspiring.

AUGUST 24

Most of us do not realize the power of faith in helping people to be what God meant them to be and to be what they themselves want to be. By the power of God anybody can be freed of any weakness; anyone can be released to creative living, no matter what difficulties stand in their way.

MAY 10

We have to learn to retain inner serenity, inner quiet, what the Quakers call "peace at the center." In order to have sustained inner strength, inner peace is needed.

A heart at peace gives life to the body.

PROVERBS 14:30

AUGUST 23

When a mother possesses serenity, kindness, feminine vitality, and spirituality, there is about her an indefinable charm which is beautiful.

MAY 11

To relax muscle tensions, practice thinking generously. If someone has not treated you right, think some generous thoughts about him and see how relaxed this makes you feel. Resentful, ill-will thoughts tighten you up. Generous thoughts loosen your entire nervous mechanism.

AUGUST 22

Faith is available to everyone. It does not make any difference what difficulty you have: physical, mental, spiritual, business, or moral; if you will begin to bear upon it—the power of faith without doubt—it can be solved.

Show this same diligence to the very end, in order to make your hope sure…imitate those who through faith and patience inherit what has been promised.

HEBREWS 6:11,12

MAY 12

It is impossible to yield to a temptation and not suffer to some degree a loss of self-respect. This subtracts from the keen sense of happiness one enjoys with full control of themselves.

AUGUST 21

If you forget those things which are behind, as the Bible teaches, and reach forward toward those things which are ahead, "pressing toward the mark for the prize of the high calling of God in Christ Jesus," you have a future that is full of strength and hope and joy.

MAY 13

When you feel tense or restless, allow these words to pass unhindered through your thoughts: "Peace I leave with you, my peace I give you...do not let your hearts be troubled and do not be afraid" (John 14:27). Conceive of these words as spreading a healing balm throughout your mind. This profound depth therapy is required to attain healing quietness.

AUGUST 20

Jesus, the Master, came back to His native village and the local people were astonished by His wisdom and His mighty works; but they did not believe. They suffered the tragedy of the closed mind. Among other villages their faith was so great that they believed if they could simply touch the edge of His garment they would be healed...and they were.

According to your faith will it be done to you.

MATTHEW 9:29

MAY 14

Human beings develop best in an environment of naturalness and affection. The best method is simply to treat teenagers as people; this means giving them respect, confidence, and pleasant comradeship. Young people have a strong, sensible streak and usually respond.

AUGUST 19

A Prayer of Forgiveness

Lord, you tell us to forgive. I do not know how to forgive. Deliver me first from the hateful pleasure of nursing a grudge—it only brings misery upon me. Help me to want to forgive. Let me know the joy of forgiveness. Amen.

MAY 15

Two qualities combine to make you strong—quietness and confidence. Deep inner quietness, the kind the Lord gives, will enable you to meet any problem calmly and solve it rightly.

In repentance and rest is your salvation,
in quietness and trust is your strength.

ISAIAH 30:15

AUGUST 18

God is the source of all energy, of all forms of life...it is a great source of peace and comfort to focus our minds on the thought that God is continually sustaining us with His love, continually ready to revitalize our souls.

MAY 16

Make each irritation in life an object of prayer. Instead of trying to destroy all of your anger, which is a consolidated force, snip away at each annoyance that feeds it by prayer. In doing so, you weaken anger and presently gain control over it.

AUGUST 17

We have only to put our problems before God with a humble and faithful heart; to believe with the simple faith of a little child, and we are promised His guidance and help.

God is our refuge and strength, an ever-present help in trouble.

PSALM 46:1

MAY 17

A Prayer When We Are Hurt

Lord, I have been hurt. Perhaps I should be less sensitive, but I have been wounded by the action of another and I must admit that I am upset and unhappy by this unkindness. Help me to forget it, to rise above it and not make more of it than the facts justify. Help me not to carry hurt anymore. Amen.

AUGUST 16

We cease being part of the world's problem and become part of the world's cure when we accept personal responsibility for doing all we can to change our private world through active faith in God.

MAY 18

We have a tendency to greatly underestimate ourselves and each other. There is actual greatness latent in each of us. Nothing makes for stronger, more enthusiastic love of life than to motivate this latent greatness and release it into action.

I can do everything through him who gives me strength.

PHILIPPIANS 4:13

AUGUST 15

The acquiring of dynamic faith is accomplished by prayer, more prayer, and by reading and mentally absorbing the Bible and practicing its prayer techniques.

The prayer of a righteous man is powerful and effective.

JAMES 5:16

MAY 19

These three remain: faith, hope, and love. Build hope into your philosophy. Hope that the difficulties will pass. Hope that the storms will cease. Hope that the pain will cease. Hope that the weakness will be overcome. In all things, keep hope.

AUGUST 14

Christianity is entirely practical. It is astounding how defeated persons can be changed into victorious individuals when they actually utilize their faith as a workable instrument. There is no situation in which faith in God will not help.

MAY 20

We should never write anything off as impossible or as a failure. God gave us the mental capacity to think our way through any problem, and the hopeful thinker projects hope and faith into the darkest situation and lights it up.

For God, who said, "Let light shine out of darkness," made his light shine in our hearts to give us the light of the knowledge of the glory of God in the face of Christ.

2 CORINTHIANS 4:6

AUGUST 13

To resent means to re-hurt. Nothing is more self-destructive than harboring resentment. I am causing myself pain by holding this feeling. Maybe I can argue that I am justified in my feeling, but even if I am, I must admit my resentment, then ask the Lord to give me a sense of forgiveness and lift me above petty things.

MAY 21

Romans 8:24 says, "We are saved by hope." If we have hope in God, we are saved to eternity. If we have hope in life, we are saved from many a defeat and many a weakness. Nestle that passage up against your heart.

AUGUST 12

Parents should be the kind of people that kids can gripe with and not about.

Fathers, do not exasperate your children; instead, bring them up in the training and instruction of the Lord.

EPHESIANS 6:4

MAY 22

People who have the quality of hope keep on going no matter what. Hope gives courage, strength, vitality, power; and somehow hopeful people always seem to win through.

May the God of hope fill you with all joy and peace as you trust in him, so that you may overflow with hope by the power of the Holy Spirit.

ROMANS 15:13

AUGUST 11

One of the best ways in which a family can erase a gap, or for that matter prevent its appearing in the first place, is to act together as a team. Bring family and business problems to the family team, for anything that is important to one is equally important to all.

MAY 23

Do all you can about a thing and, having done all, turn it over to God; leave it with Him; rest it with Him confidently, prayerfully, and with faith. He may not give you the answer you want, but He will give you the answer you should have. He will always do what is right for you.

AUGUST 10

When a child is not disciplined he is thereby denied his basic heritage. You can count on it that he will be disciplined by the world, and it will not be with the kind of love that should exist within the family.

Discipline your son, for in that there is hope.

PROVERBS 19:18

MAY 24

Sound Christian morality is vital to full emotional health.

Be careful to obey so that it may go well with you and that you may increase greatly in a land flowing with milk and honey, just as the Lord...promised you.

DEUTERONOMY 6:3

AUGUST 9

A true father's responsibility does not diminish but, rather, increases in proportion to a child's needs. At its best fatherhood is everlastingly creative.

MAY 25

There are times when the path of righteousness can seem the loneliest place in the world. When such loneliness comes upon you, remember that you are not really alone. God is with you. If your loneliness is the result of some difficult but honorable choice, He knows about it, and loves you for it.

AUGUST 8

Start preparing for happy old age when you are young. If you are tight with money at thirty you will be a miser at seventy. If you talk a lot at thirty you will be a windbag at seventy. If you are kind and thoughtful at thirty you will be lovable at seventy.

MAY 26

There are ways to overcome loneliness. Show an interest in other lonely people. Study yourself to discover why you have so few friends. Get some sparkle into your conversation. Develop a prayer list and pray every day for those on your list and look for opportunities to bring encouragement, especially to those who suffer.

AUGUST 7

When the mind is filled with the Lord's presence, the mind is automatically filled with light. Fears that lurk among shadows and thrive in darkness are driven off.

The Lord is my light and my salvation—
whom shall I fear?
The Lord is the stronghold of my life—
of whom shall I be afraid?

PSALM 27:1

MAY 27

The gospel of Jesus Christ is a healing agency; the holy words give you not only philosophical understanding, ethical perception, moral values, and strength, but they also have healing power. There is healing in His words.

Man does not live on bread alone but on every word that comes from the mouth of the Lord.

DEUTERONOMY 8:3

AUGUST 6

This country was made great by people who struggled; and if it is to be great in the future, that too will be due to the same kind of people.

MAY 28

Every medical doctor is familiar with the strength-giving powers of hope. Dr. Harold G. Wolff reported that it is a medical fact that when a man has hope he is "capable of enduring incredible burdens and taking cruel punishment."

AUGUST 5

The Bible does not promise immunity from trouble, suffering, or sorrow, but it does offer the power to meet these fearlessly, serenely, and creatively.

MAY 29

The real sickness of man is in his mind and in his soul. It is this disharmony which Jesus makes whole. When we seek to touch Him, really seek to touch Him, power will come out of Him and we too shall be healed.

When she heard about Jesus, she came up behind him in the crowd and touched his cloak, because she thought, "If I just touch his clothes, I will be healed."

MARK 5:27,28

AUGUST 4

You cannot overcome a fear by pretending you don't have it. You can be rid of it by invoking the powerful force of faith to displace it.

When I am afraid, I will trust in you. In God, whose word I praise, in God I trust; I will not be afraid.

PSALM 56:3,4

MAY 30

Prayer for Healing

Dear Lord, I believe in Your power to heal the sick. Through faith—the tremendous healing force of God the Creator re-creates. I hold our loved one up to You and humbly ask that You will lay Your hands upon him and restore him.

AUGUST 3

In an age where external controls have grown weak or are actually disappearing, the individual must set up his own standards and you, as an individual, can do it. Choose the higher path. Choose the more difficult goal. The preacher can preach, the moralist can exhort, but nothing will happen unless the individual says to himself, "I choose."

MAY 31

During the day we pick up mental odds and ends: a little worry, a little resentment, a few annoyances, perhaps even some guilt reactions. Every night these should be thrown out, for unless eliminated they accumulate.

AUGUST 2

Jesus Christ is still the greatest healer. There is healing in His words. He heals the brokenhearted and binds up their wounds.

PSALM 147:3

JUNE 1

Being full of fear for a loved one who needs healing may interfere with or obstruct the healing process. An attitude of faith and love releases a sick person more fully into the flow of healing power and is an important influence in bringing about a state of well-being.

Don't be afraid, just believe.... The child is not dead but asleep.... Little girl, I say to you, get up!

MARK 5:36,39,41

AUGUST 1

The two words "deny yourself" are the very essence of self-control. Don't consider it a decision "against" some form of fun, but a decision "for" a desired goal in your life.

JUNE 2

Every person, if he is to have mental health and live successfully, must move away from past failures and mistakes and go forward without letting them be a weight upon him. The art of forgetting is absolutely necessary.

JULY 31

It is an absolute, demonstrable fact that the person who really practices love—real love—rises so high above fear that it can no longer touch him. Where love is, fear cannot live. Love withers fear.

There is no fear in love. But perfect love drives out fear.

1 JOHN 4:18

JUNE 3

Continue to bless and love people whom you may dislike or resent. Gradually, your new attitude of love will penetrate the subconscious, ultimately displacing the hate thoughts. Then you will be released from ill will and you will attain the wonderful spiritual achievement of forgiveness.

Bless those who curse you, pray for those who mistreat you.

LUKE 6:28

JULY 30

You need not fear if you know an action is right. If you pray about it and feel the presence of God, there is nothing in this world that can defeat you. It may go hard; you may receive blows, but God will not let you down. He will see you through.

JUNE 4

There is something almost intangible about complete honesty, complete integrity. When you encounter it in a person you know it, and you know you can trust him. This ability to inspire trust and confidence is often a factor in their success.

JULY 29

Move away from past failures and mistakes and go forward without letting them be a weight upon you. Every night when you lie down to sleep practice dropping the day into the past. Look confidently to the future with God.

Because of the Lord's great love we are not consumed, for his compassions never fail. They are new every morning; great is your faithfulness.

LAMENTATIONS 3:22,23

JUNE 5

The solution to my inferiority complex was in finding a personal relationship with Christ. The result was so satisfying that, in my enthusiasm, I wanted to share my discovery with everyone else.

JULY 28

Once having told your troubles to a competent counselor or to God and having been forgiven by God and having found release, then fully forgive yourself and turn your back definitely on these troubles; have faith and go forward.

JUNE 6

*As long as you hate a person, they have power over you.
They can upset you. They can make your life miserable.
But if you love them, they lose this power.
They no longer control the situation.*

Love your enemies, do good to those who hate you...
do to others as you would have them do to you.

LUKE 6:27,31

JULY 27

There is something triumphantly final about getting to the phase of overcoming petty tyrants, like smoking and drinking, simply because "we make up our mind" to get rid of them altogether. Nobody forces us or directs us...the direction comes from within and we simply make up our minds about it.

JUNE 7

My mother once spoke to me about ambition. She said, "It is good if God controls it…but what I want you to be is a clean, decent, honorable, upright Christian man with love in your heart, serving God and His children, and I want you to so live that when you finish your course of life…I'll meet you somewhere in the eternities of our Lord."

JULY 26

God has given man the power of private judgment. In the life of the human being there is nothing fully predictable. A man can alter his environment and change his future because God has given him a will of his own and left it free.

To man belong the plans of the heart, but from the Lord comes the reply of the tongue.... Commit to the Lord whatever you do, and your plans will succeed.

PROVERBS 16:1,3

JUNE 8

It is healthy to forgive, to say nothing of it being the right way to live. Develop the habit of looking for people's good points. Everybody has them.

Be kind and compassionate to one another, forgiving each other, just as in Christ God forgave you.

EPHESIANS 4:32

JULY 25

One of the most important factors in success and happiness is the ability to make friends. The rare faculty of being able to satisfactorily adjust to those around you is demanded of all those who would live effective lives.

JUNE 9

To be successful in daily living, a person must know himself. He should objectively consider his attributes and liabilities and be willing to change his ways. Before a person can know other people and understand the world about him, he must first of all understand and know himself.

JULY 24

I believe that if a person will seriously get acquainted with Jesus Christ and absorb His Spirit and attitude, he can master the art of making and keeping friends.

Love each other as I have loved you. Greater love has no one than this, that he lay down his life for his friends.

JOHN 15:12,13

JUNE 10

Changing one's thought pattern is a long and difficult process which is accomplished by the practice of displacing unhealthy thoughts with creative attitudes.

JULY 23

Every one of us needs to learn the art of getting along well with other people. When differences arise, do something about them quickly. There is something in human nature that seems to delight in magnifying differences when they arise. Settle them and get down to the unity between oneself and others.

JUNE 11

The person who practices redemptive love finds it for himself and contributes it to everybody else. This kind of love changes people's lives and changes the world.

He has rescued us from the dominion of darkness
and brought us into the kingdom of the Son
he loves, in whom we have redemption,
the forgiveness of sins.

COLOSSIANS 1:13,14

JULY 22

A true friend knows when you need a word of affection and encouragement. He is one of those thoughtful people who is sensitive, or tuned in, to the hearts and minds of others.

JUNE 12

Before you can really like other people you must like yourself. Jesus said, "Love your neighbor as yourself," indicating that liking one's self is the standard for liking others.

JULY 21

If you are having misunderstandings with anybody, list the points of unity you have with them...then underscore the points of agreement rather than your differences.

Love must be sincere.... Be devoted to one another in brotherly love. Honor one another above yourselves.

ROMANS 12:9,10

JUNE 13

Storms bring out the eagles while little birds take to cover. Every child of God has eagle characteristics in them. Eagles ride out the storms to better things. The storms help grow strong wings.

Those who hope in the Lord will renew their strength. They will soar on wings like eagles; they will run and not grow weary, they will walk and not faint.

ISAIAH 40:31

JULY 20

Don't ride life too hard. It is not necessary for any human being to live in frustration—nor allow himself to become old, worn, tired, disgusted. He has opportunity, if he will open his mind and heart, to live life that is dynamic and exciting. "Let the peace of Christ rule in your hearts." You can rule over frustration by the peace of Christ in your heart.

JUNE 14

The greatest step forward in self-improvement is through spiritual experience. A man can no more change himself by himself than a leopard can change its spots. The real art of self-improvement is Christ improvement. He effects the change in you.

JULY 19

The healing of stress is peace.

For [Christ] himself is our peace...and in him you too are being built together to become a dwelling in which God lives by his Spirit.

EPHESIANS 2:14,22

JUNE 15

If you can't be with a sorrowing friend or relative, it helps to express your feelings by writing or sending a flower or simply offering to do something useful.

Mourn with those who mourn.

ROMANS 12:15

JULY 18

All normal children possess in infancy qualities of genius. Mediocrity, apparently, does not appear until later in life.

JUNE 16

No matter how much psychiatric counseling one receives, and regardless of the quality of such guidance, the ultimate fact is that every person, on his own, by himself, with God's help must take that final decisive step that activates the cure of unhealthy mental patterns.

JULY 17

Reject hopelessness; substitute faith; use intelligent, persevering effort and you can lift yourself out of hopelessness.

Now faith is being sure of what we hope for and certain of what we do not see.

HEBREWS 11:1

JUNE 17

The secret of being happy is to have something in your heart that lifts you above the contrary, the pain, the frustration and defeats of human life.

Do not let your hearts be troubled. Trust in God, trust also in Me...I will come back and take you to be with Me.

JOHN 14:1,3

JULY 16

God gives himself to the profoundly sincere and to the deeply desiring.... God will come into your life when you want Him with all your heart.... The moment you give God your whole self...He will come to you and help you as you have never dreamed possible.

JUNE 18

Get a new image of yourself as a child of God having greater possibilities than have ever appeared. Don't self-limit your possibilities even in your private thoughts.

JULY 15

*P*ut something of yourself into everything you give. A gift, however great or small, speaks its own language. And when it tells of the love of the giver, it is truly blessed.

Freely you have received, freely give.

MATTHEW 10:8

JUNE 19

My father taught me a great truth that has added much joy to my life. "To treat each man as a child of God is the big secret of happy living," he said. "Hold him in esteem and it will make him and you happy." The way you think about people, how you treat them and react to them, is extremely important to your own happiness.

Love one another. As I have loved you.

JOHN 13:34

JULY 14

In my counseling with people who seek help in meeting life more effectively, I have found that their basic need is simply to find God.

JUNE 20

How do you go about being a happy person? Get into God's rhythm. Rhythm is another word for harmony, and harmony is another word for joy. Therefore, when you are joyful, you are in rhythm.

JULY 13

Many people fail in life because they have no sense of direction, no system, no guiding principles. They have no major cause or beliefs to give meaning to life.

Jesus answered, "I am the way and the truth and the life."

JOHN 14:6

JUNE 21

The happy person is the person who keeps his faith, who believes and endures until the morning—and the morning always comes.

JULY 12

God who created us also continuously re-creates us. He who gave us life gives us the gift of life continuing. Our power to move, act, grow, progress, and accomplish is from God. Through God our life has meaning.

JUNE 22

Even if you could correct all the problems in the world, that would not necessarily create happiness. Happiness is of the inner spirit; it is the ability to perceive and experience that which is beautiful, fine, and exquisite.

May the righteous be glad and rejoice before God; may they be happy and joyful.

PSALM 68:3

JULY 11

A doctor once told me: "I am a surgeon, not a psychiatrist, but I have cured more people by treating their souls than I have with a knife. About seventy-five percent of my patients do not really need medicine as much as they need God. They are all searching for something only God can give."

JUNE 23

Take a good straight look at yourself and dare to realize that amazing powers are within you. One of the most important things is to go beyond merely being kindly and considerate, as splendid as that is, and start really loving and esteeming people in an active out-going manner. Do not be content to just be good, be good for something.

JULY 10

*Show me a man who really knows God
and I will show you a happy,
enthusiastic and vital man.*

I consider everything a loss compared
to the surpassing greatness of knowing
Christ Jesus my Lord.

PHILIPPIANS 3:8

JUNE 24

The Bible is filled with statements about joy and happiness...but happiness does not come easily. Often you may have to struggle for it.

Praise the Lord, O my soul, and forget not all his benefits—who forgives all your sins and heals all your diseases, who redeems your life from the pit and crowns you with love and compassion, who satisfies your desires with good things.

PSALM 103:2,4,5

JULY 9

Out of His abundance God gives more than we can ask or think, according to the "power that works in us." You get this power by receiving it from God, who gives it through faith in Jesus Christ. When you receive this inner power…there is nothing in the world that you cannot overcome.

JUNE 25

Members of a service club in one city went out to give a dollar to every person on the street who looked happy. At day's end they had been able to give away only thirty-three dollars. Perhaps life is getting so impersonal that people feel insignificant and retreat into their shells. Or are we taking life too seriously?

JULY 8

God is a loving God. He loves you more dearly than your mother or your father loves you. You are His child. Get to know Him and trust His love.

How great is the love the Father has lavished on us, that we should be called children of God!

1 JOHN 3:1

JUNE 26

The Constitution, like the Bible, is applicable to problems of any time or circumstance. Even in today's affluent, sophisticated world, the Constitution is as fresh and modern as tomorrow's newspaper.

JULY 7

God is great. He is the God who threw all the stars and planets out into illimitable space and has them perfectly ordered. You hear Him in the thunder; you see Him in the clouds; you see Him in the might of science—a wonderful God.

JUNE 27

If your predicament looks hopeless, remember there is no situation so completely black that something constructive cannot be done about it. When faced with a minus, ask what you can do to make it a plus.

With God all things are possible.
MATTHEW 19:26

JULY 6

There is no circumstance in your life where God will not stand with you and help you, no matter what it is. He understands all your troubles, all your frustrations and disappointments. He understands your weaknesses. He loves you.

JUNE 28

In 1776 the country was aflame with patriotism during the Fourth of July. Today it's a day of golf, swimming, and picnics. There is always a danger that, after the passing of time, great events become minimized and linger amongst us only in formalities that do not in any sense express the original power that gave rise to them.

JULY 5

To make the day good you will need to see it in your mind as good. We become what we think.

We know that in all things God works for the good of those who love him, who have been called according to his purpose.

ROMANS 8:28

JULY 1

Great events are born in white heat. Today we have freedom and liberty but we do not remember that men fought and died to attain it. Blood flowed and anguish was suffered to give us liberty. Now on sacred days of freedom we mumble a few polite words with no deep realization of the content of the thing we celebrate.

JULY 2